Playing with Scales

A FRESH WAY TO PRACTISE SCALES!

VIOLIN

LEVEL ONE

Devised and arranged
by Alistair Watson

CHESTER MUSIC
part of The Music Sales Group
London / New York / Paris / Sydney / Copenhagen /
Berlin / Madrid / Hong Kong / Tokyo

Published by
Chester Music
14-15 Berners Street, London W1T 3LJ, UK.

Exclusive Distributors:
Music Sales Limited
Distribution Centre, Newmarket Road,
Bury St Edmunds, Suffolk IP33 3YB, UK.
Music Sales Pty Limited
Units 3-4, 17 Willfox Street, Condell Park,
NSW 2200, Australia.

Order No. CH82060
ISBN: 978-1-78305-290-5
This book © Copyright 2014 Wise Publications,
a division of Music Sales Limited.

Edited by Jenni Norey.
Devised and arranged by Alistair Watson.
Cover design by Fresh Lemon.
Printed in the EU.

Playing With Scales: The Concept

Playing With Scales is a new educational resource designed to help young musicians play their scales. It consists of a series of fun accompaniments for scales and arpeggios, written to cover the keys and scale patterns required by the instrument. Teachers can accompany their students in lessons and then students can practise their scales at home with audio downloaded using the unique card enclosed in the back of the book.

Playing With Scales can help the student in several ways. Playing over an accompaniment will help with timing, as part of the challenge with playing scales is to get them to flow evenly from one note to the next.

Intonation will also benefit. Most importantly of all, the actual experience of playing scales will be enriched. Scales will no longer feel dry and disembodied, as they now become part of a piece of music. The accompaniments have been written in a wide variety of styles, to suit all tastes and moods. Various tonalities are also explored. Some accompaniments are not even in the same key as the scale; a major scale can sit quite nicely over an accompaniment that is in the relative minor, for example. The aim of *Playing With Scales* is to engage the imagination of the student, and ultimately, *to make scale practice fun!*

Playing With Scales: Violin, Level One

This volume contains accompaniments for scales and arpeggios required at the first level of playing. Each scale has a series of accompaniments, which present the student with a range of different styles and moods. All the accompaniments are available as audio downloads, but can also be played by a teacher in lessons. *Playing With Scales* therefore becomes an interactive tool for use in a student's lesson.

C major scale

Straight notes

Long tonic

C major arpeggio

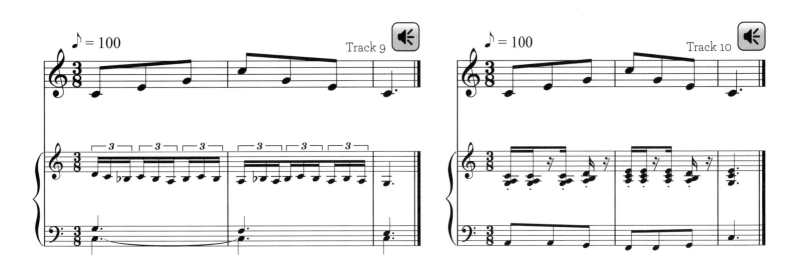

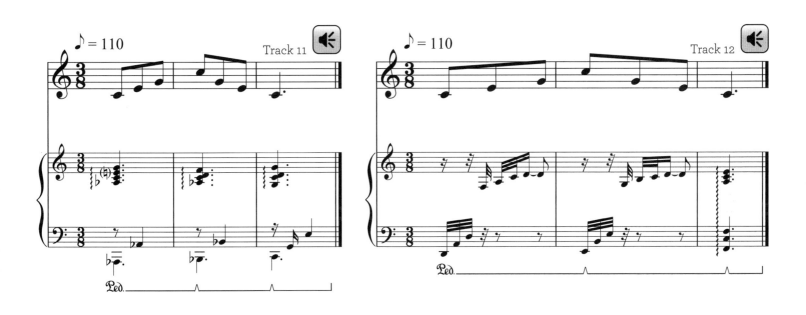

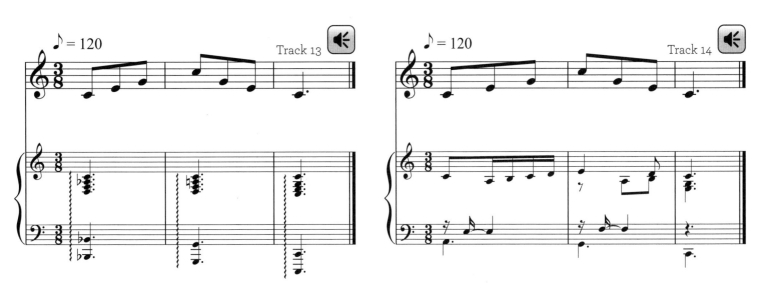

9

D major scale

Straight notes

Long tonic

11

D major arpeggio

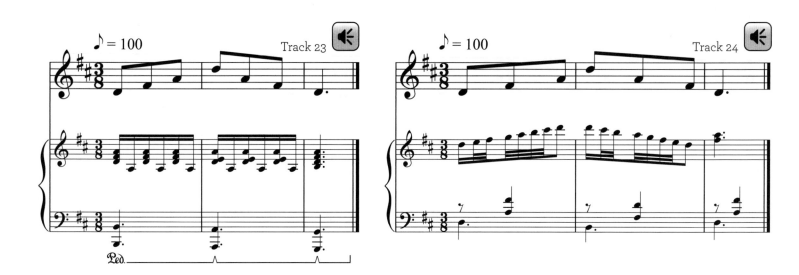

Track 23

Track 24

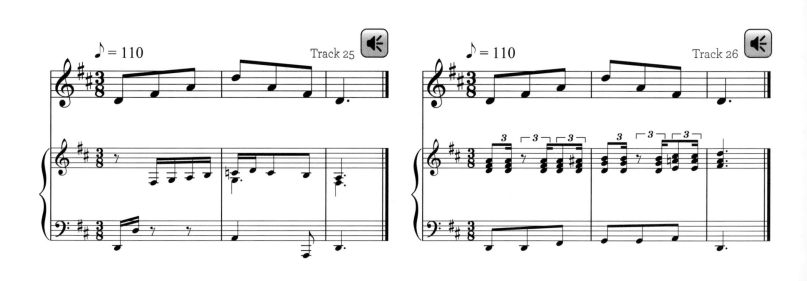

Track 25

Track 26

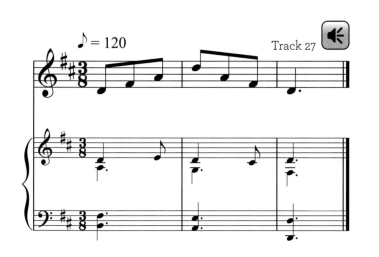

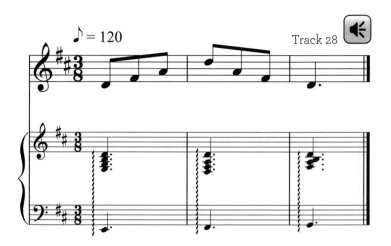

Track 27

Track 28

G major scale

Straight notes

Straight notes

Long tonic

Long tonic

G major arpeggio

A major scale

Straight notes

Track 41

Track 42

Track 43

Track 44

Long tonic

A major arpeggio

E minor scale

Straight notes

Track 55

Track 56

Track 57

Track 58

21

Long tonic

E minor arpeggio

Track 63
Track 64

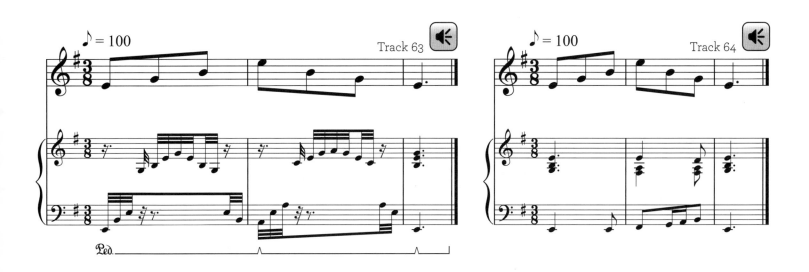

Track 65
Track 66

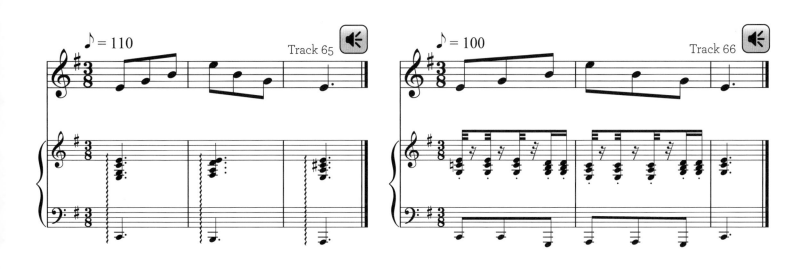

Track 67
Track 68

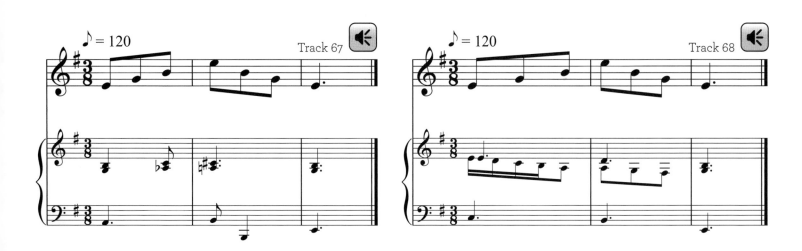

123456789

HOW TO DOWNLOAD YOUR MUSIC TRACKS

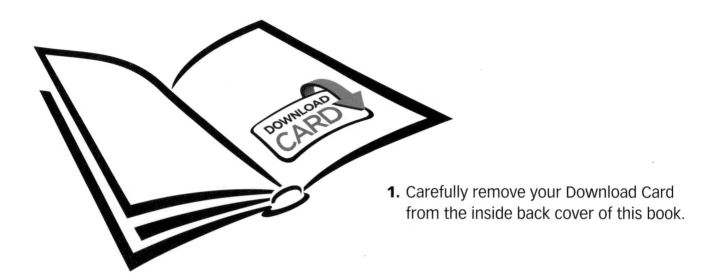

1. Carefully remove your Download Card from the inside back cover of this book.

TO REDEEM THIS CARD VISIT
www.musicsalesdownloads.com

ENTER ACCESS CODE:

XXXXXXXXX

Download Cards are powered by Dropcards.
User must accept terms at dropcards.com/terms
which are adopted by The Music Sales Group.
Not reedemable for cash. Void where prohibited or restricted by law.

DCARD1006478

2. On the back of the card is your unique access code. Enter this at www.musicsalesdownloads.com

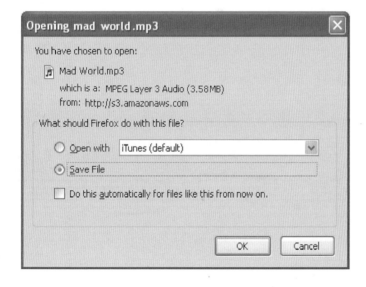

3. Follow the instructions to save your files to your computer*. That's it!

*Appearance of download manager will vary depending upon operating system and web browser.
In case of difficulty when downloading files, please contact dropcards.com/help
Card missing? Please contact music@musicsales.co.uk